GW00384641

Learning Stars
Pupil's Book 2

Contents

Jeanne Perrett and Jill Leighton

Unit Topic	Phonics and handwriting	Vocabulary	Language / Grammar	Development concepts	Life skills
1 My house	Alphabet review	KEY VOCABULARY L1 – bedroom, bathroom, living room, kitchen, garden, house ADDITIONAL VOC – soap, towel, wash	Review of Level 1: I've got ..., I like ..., This is ...	clean and dirty	I can wash my face
2 My day	Letter sounds and names Short vowel sounds: a, e, i, o, u	KEY VOCABULARY L1 & 2 – get up, have breakfast, go to school, have lunch, go home, play, have dinner, go to bed ADDITIONAL VOC – days of the week	Present simple for routines	identifying their favourite day	I can get up on time
3 My favourite food	'a' cvc words: hat, cat, bat, rat, fat, mat, tap, jam, pan, van, dad, sad	KEY VOCABULARY L1 – chicken, salad, rice, fish, mangoes, oranges, cucumber, beans, aubergine, favourite ADDITIONAL VOC – taste, hear, see, smell, touch	Do you like ...? Yes, I do/ No, I don't.	identifying their favourite food/taste	I can wash my hands before I eat
4 At the zoo	'e' & 'i' cvc words: ten, pen, hen, red, bed, peg, wig, dig, big, pin, tin, sit	KEY VOCABULARY L1 – tigers, lions, giraffes, elephants, kangaroos, penguins, monkeys ADDITIONAL VOC – leaves, meat, fish, grass, bananas, bamboo	Present simple they form: They eat ... They like ... Do they ...?	classifying animals	I can get ready to go out
5 My weekend	'o' & 'u' cvc words: hot, pot, dog, hot, box, fox, jug, cup, nut, cut, sun, bus	KEY VOCABULARY L1 – cousins, aunt, uncle, happy, sad, tired, excited ADDITIONAL VOC – numbers one-twelve	Where are they? They're behind/next to the ... What's the time? It's ... o'clock	discriminating between places; expressing their feelings	I can go to bed on time
6 My town	'u' cvc words: mum, yum, rug, hug, mud, hut, bun, mug, run	KEY VOCABULARY L1 – shops, supermarket, library, cinema, café, museum, pool ADDITIONAL VOC – straight on, turn left, turn right	Where do you want to go? To the museum.	left and right; following directions	I can say my address
7 My favourite clothes	'sh' words: ship, shop, shut, shell, shorts, shelf, dish, splash, fish	KEY VOCABULARY L1 – swimsuit, swimming trunks, sandals, dress, shirt, jeans, armbands ADDITIONAL VOC – spring, summer, autumn, winter	Present continuous: What are you wearing? I'm wearing ...	big and small; matching clothes to seasons	I can get dressed by myself
8 Jobs	'll' & 'ck' words: smell, bell, shell, hill, fill, doll, black, snack, stick, sock, clock, duck	KEY VOCABULARY L1 – firefighter, police officer, doctor, nurse, dentist, engineer ADDITIONAL VOC – toothpaste, toothbrush	What do you want to be? I want to be ...	clean and dirty; making sensible choices	I can clean my teeth
9 Transport	'ch' & 'th' words: chick, chip, chicken, chin, lunch, munch, thin, thick, bath, path	KEY VOCABULARY L1 – bus, train, plane, boat, helicopter, taxi, coach ADDITIONAL VOC – sink, float	We can go by ... or ...	following instructions	I can wear my seat belt
10 Little Red Riding Hood	Review of all phonics words	KEY VOCABULARY L1 – Little Red Riding Hood, wolf, Grandma, flowers, birds ADDITIONAL VOC – We play music. We sing and dance. We make puppets. We paint big pictures. We make masks.	Review	cooperation; identifying odd-one-out	We can work together

Songs and chants	Maths skills	Cross-curricular themes	Story and drama	Review
New vocabulary chant Where are you? song The alphabet song	Numbers: 1–10; Counting; Fine motor skills; Visual discrimination; Next in a sequence; Matching; Understanding quantity; Bar chart; Shape vocabulary: square, triangle, rectangle circle	PSHE: Healthy habits/routines (wash your hands)	I like baths	Letters: Aa–Zz. Words: ant, bird, cat, dog duck , elephant, fish, gorilla, hippo, insect, jellyfish, kangaroo, lion, monkey, nurse, octopus, parrot, queen bee, rabbit, snake, tiger, umbrella bird, vulture, worm, ox, yak, zebra
New vocabulary chant What do you do? song Alphabet chant Clap your hands song Cat in a hat song Days of the week song	Numbers: 11 and 12; Addition; Visual discrimination; Next in a sequence; Counting; Fine motor skills; Matching; Shapes; Join the numbers; Colour by number; Subtraction	PSHE: days of the week; weekend	Play day	Words: cat, hat, Ted, bed, pin, tin, dog, log, run, sun Language: I've got; I like; This is Colours
New vocabulary chant What's your favourite food? song	Time; Visual discrimination; Reading clock face; Fine motor skills; Vocabulary: daily routine; Visual discrimination; Join the numbers; Next in a sequence	PSHE: the five senses	In the restaurant with Grandma and Grandpa	Words: eyes, ears, nose, fingers Is he in the ...? What do you do on ...?
New vocabulary chant What can animals do? song	Numbers: 13, 14 and 15; Addition; Visual discrimination; Counting; Fine motor skills; Understanding quantity; Next in a sequence; Shapes; Colour by number	Science: What animals eat	My bananas!	
New vocabulary chant Are you happy? song	Numbers: 16, 17 and 18; Addition; Visual discrimination; Fine motor skills; Counting; Tally marks; Colour by number; Understanding quantity; Next in a sequence; Shapes: star	PSHE: o' clock times	Hide and seek	Numbers
New vocabulary chant What do you want to do today? song	Numbers: 19 and 20; Addition; Visual discrimination; Fine motor skills; Matching; Counting; Next in a sequence; Subtraction; Join the numbers; Understanding quantity	PE: moving in different directions	Where do you want to go?	What are they? They're ... Do they eat ...? They're behind/next to ...
New vocabulary chant What are you wearing today? song The seasons song Small waves, big waves song	Numbers: 20–30; Addition; Fine motor skills; Counting; Estimation; Visual discrimination; Shapes; Next in a sequence; Bar chart	Science: Seasons – weather	Small waves and big waves!	
New vocabulary chant What do you want to be? song	Counting in 10s to 100; Addition; Fine motor skills; Estimation; Subtraction; Visual discrimination; Vocabulary: bigger and smaller; Colour by number	PSHE – Looking after your teeth	I want to be a doctor	Present simple I want to be ...
New vocabulary chant How can we go? song Boats float song	Even numbers: 2–20; Counting; Fine motor skills; Visual discrimination; Next in a sequence; Shapes; Addition; Subtraction; Estimation	Science: Experiment – sink or float?	Do boats float?	
	Review; Bar chart; Counting; Visual discrimination; Fine motor skills; Next in a sequence; Addition; Estimation; Join the numbers; Colour by number	Drama: Backstage – making, painting and craft activities	The school show	I'm ..., We're ..., What are you wearing today? I'm wearing my ...? What do you want to be? I want to be a ... Can we go by ...? We can go home by ...

Unit 1
Lesson 1

My house

I are my like the with is

in can a and

garden

1 **2**

bathroom

bedroom

living room

kitchen

I like my **house!**

3

This is my **bedroom.**

4

This is the bedroom.

I can ...

I can wash my face.

 1    2

3   4

New Words

4

Listen and chant.
Listen, point and repeat.
Listen.
Play.

5

6

Where's Horsey?

Dad is in the **living room**.

Mum is in the **kitchen**.

Grandma and Grandpa
are in the **garden**.

Horsey is in the **bathroom**!

7

 **5**
 6
7

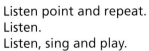
Listen point and repeat.
Listen.
Listen, sing and play.

 **Grammar** Review of Level 1

 **About me!** What's your favourite room?

 5

a b c d e f g h i j k l

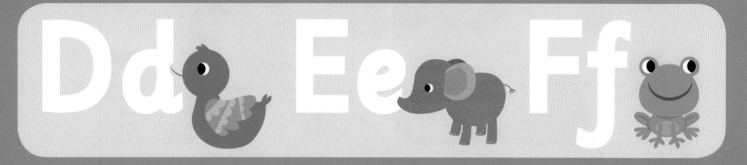

A a   B b   C c

D d   E e   F f

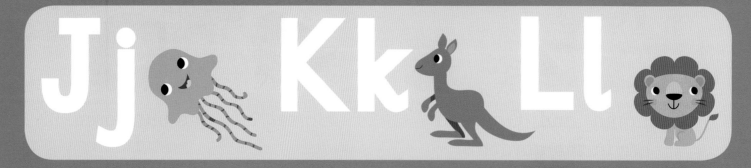

G g   H h   I i

J j   K k   L l

Listen.
Sing: *The alphabet song.*
Play: *I spy.*
Play: *Animal clues.*

Mm Nn Oo

Pp Qq Rr Ss

Tt Uu Vv

Ww Xx Yy Zz

5 6 7

Listen.
Sing: *The alphabet song.*
Play: *Letter sound, picture and name game.*

Wash your hands

Eat with clean hands.

Wash your hands. Use soap.

Rinse your hands.

Dry your hands.
Use a clean towel.

1

2

3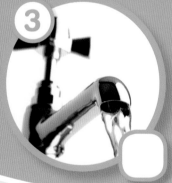

4

1    2

 PSHE

Listen and point.
Mime the actions.
Look and draw:
✓ = clean   ✗ = dirty.

 About me!

What colour
soap do you
like?

I like baths

1. I like baths.

2. A red car and a yellow duck.

3. I'm clean.

4. I can jump.

5. Help!

6. I'm dirty.

1 Listen, point and repeat.
2 Listen to the story.
3 Act out the story.

About me! Do you like baths or showers?

Unit 2 My day

1

2

What do you do every day?

I have me with the no we

get up in a on it can

I get up.

I have **breakfast**.

I go to school.

I have **lunch**.

3

 1

 2

 3

I can ...

I can get up on time.

 10

Listen and chant.
Listen, point and repeat.
Listen.

New Words

4

I go home.

I play.

I have **dinner**.

I go to bed.

5 **6**

Listen, point and repeat.
Listen.
Listen, sing and play.

 Grammar Present simple for routines.

 About me! Who do you play with?

a b c d e f g h i j k l m
n o p q r s t u v w x y z

Horsey

Bella

Jack

Lily

Listen and repeat.
Chant the alphabet.
Spell the names.
Sing: *Clap your hands song.*

12

Aa Ee Ii Oo Uu

Cat in a hat.

Ted in a bed.

Pin in a tin.

Dog on a log.

Run in the sun.

 1
 2
 3
 4

Listen and repeat.
Listen and point to the letters.
Sing: *Cat in a hat song.*
Play: *Is it a vowel?*

Days of the week

Sunday

Monday

Tuesday

Thursday

Wednesday

Friday

Saturday

1

2

3

PSHE

Listen, point and repeat.
Listen, look and say the day.
Sing.

About me!

What do you do on Saturdays?

Play day

It's Saturday.

No school today.

Can we play schools? Yes.

I'm the teacher.

We're at school, Mum.

Lunch for you.
Thank you, Mum.

Listen, point and repeat.
Listen to the story.
Act out the story.

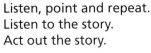

 Do you play schools
with your friends?

Unit 3 My favourite food
Lesson 1

1 2

I is my me the with

am get hello a and in

3

4

menu

chicken   salad   rice

fish   mangoes   oranges

cucumber   beans   aubergine

CAFE

I can ...

I can wash my hands before I eat.

New Words

1 😊 **2** 🎧
3 🎧 **4** 😊

16

Listen and chant.
Listen, point and repeat.
Listen.
Play.

5

What's your favourite food?   My favourite food is chicken.

6

7

What's your favourite food?

My favourite food is ...

8

 **5** **6** **7**

Listen, point and repeat.
Listen.
Say.
Sing.

8

 Grammar   *Do you like?*
Yes, I do. /
No, I don't.

About me!   What's your favourite food?

Aa

1. h → a → t hat
2. c → a → t cat
3. b → a → t bat
4. r → a → t rat
5. f → a → t fat
6. m → a → t mat
7. t → a → p tap
8. j → a → m jam
9. p → a → n pan
10. v → a → n van
11. d → a → d dad
12. s → a → d sad

1
2
3
4

Listen and point.
Listen and repeat.
Listen, point and say.
Listen. Find and say the number.

Fat Cat

1

A rat and a bat.

2

Tap, tap, tap. I am a rat with a hat. Hello, hello, hello.

3

Tap, tap, tap. I am a bat with a mat. Hello, hello, hello.

4

Tap, tap, tap. I am Fat Cat. I want a rat and a bat in my pan!

5

The jam! My pan!

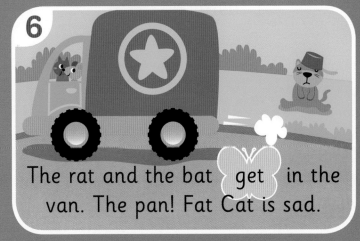

6

The rat and the bat get in the van. The pan! Fat Cat is sad.

1 **2** **3**

Listen and point to the words.
Point and repeat.
Listen and say the number.

Five senses

eyes

tongue

ears

fingers

nose

I taste

I hear

I see

I smell

I touch

PSHE

Listen, point and repeat.
Listen, point and repeat.
Listen and say.

What's your favourite taste?

Review

1

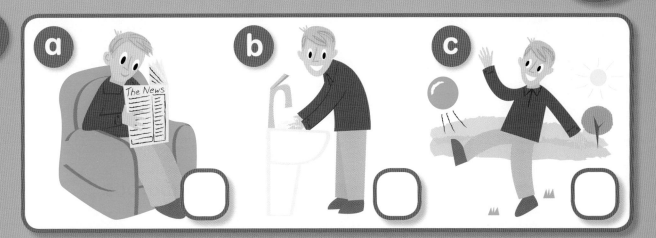

a b c

a b c

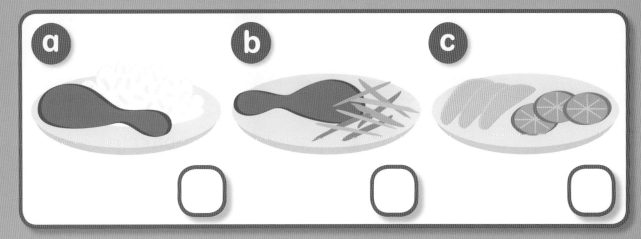

a b c

2

 1

 2

 Review

Listen and tick.
Listen, point and say.
Assess progress with
Teacher's Guide.

Unit 4 At the Zoo

Lesson 1

1 2

has I no like here the

in did and a it on

kangaroos

lions

tigers

giraffes

elephants

penguins

monkeys

3

4

I can ...

1 Listen and chant.
2 Listen, point and repeat.
3 Listen.
4 Sing.

22

New Words

I can get ready to go out.

5

6

Monkeys eat fruit.

They like bananas!

7

They're monkeys!

Listen, point and repeat.
Listen.
Play.

Present simple:
they form
They eat fruit.
They like bananas.

 What's your favourite wild animal?

 23

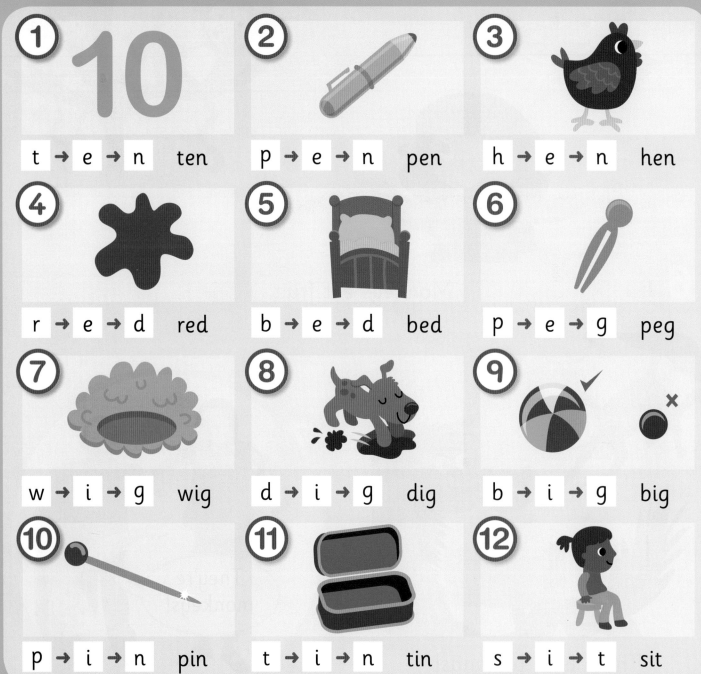

① 10 — t → e → n — ten

② — p → e → n — pen

③ — h → e → n — hen

④ — r → e → d — red

⑤ — b → e → d — bed

⑥ — p → e → g — peg

⑦ — w → i → g — wig

⑧ — d → i → g — dig

⑨ — b → i → g — big

⑩ — p → i → n — pin

⑪ — t → i → n — tin

⑫ — s → i → t — sit

Listen and point.
Listen and repeat.
Listen, point and say.
Listen. Find and say the number.

Dig, Ed, dig!

1

Dig here, Ed.

Ed has a big map.

2

Dig here, Ed.

Ed digs and digs.

3

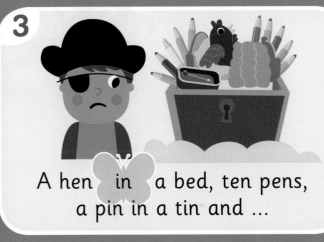

A hen in a bed, ten pens, a pin in a tin and ...

4

A map in a cap!

5

Dig here, Ed.

It's wet. Sit on the mat.

6

I did it!

You did it, Ed! You did it!

Listen and point to the words.
Point and repeat.
Listen and say the number.

What animals eat

①

tigers

② monkeys

③

penguins

④

pandas

ⓐ

meat

ⓑ

fish

ⓒ

bamboo

ⓓ

bananas

 ① ②  ③

Science

Listen, point and repeat.
Look and guess: *What do monkeys eat? They eat …*
Listen and match.

 About me!

Do you eat meat?

My bananas!

Do lions eat vegetables? No!

Do giraffes eat leaves? Yes!

Do elephants eat grass? Yes!

Do monkeys eat fruit? Yes!

I'm Horsey. I eat bananas.

Thank you!

Listen, point and repeat.
Listen to the story.
Act out the story.

 Do you eat bananas?

27

Unit 5
Lesson 1
My weekend

my are the me of no we

in it a and hello

1 2

sad

excited

tired

3

happy

my cousins

my aunt

my uncle

4

1 2 3 4

Listen and chant.
Listen, point and repeat.
Listen.
Sing.

New Words

I can ...

I can go to bed on time.

Where are they?

There!

Hello!

He's excited.

Where are they?

They're behind the bag!

Listen, point and repeat.
Listen.
Play.

 Grammar

*Where are they?
They're behind /
next to the …*

 About me!

Have you got a cousin?

29

5 Lesson 3   Oo Uu

1 h → o → t   hot

2 p → o → t   pot

3 d → o → g   dog

4 h → o → p   hop

5 b → o → x   box

6 f → o → x   fox

7 j → u → g   jug

8 c → u → p   cup

9 n → u → t   nut

10 c → u → t   cut

11 s → u → n   sun

12 b → u → s   bus

1   **2**   **3**   **4**

Listen and point.
Listen and repeat.
Listen, point and say.
Listen. Find and say the number.

Bob has a job

1

Bob has a job. Hello, Bob! Hello, Gus the gorilla. It's hot in the sun.

2

A big jug of milk and six cups!

3

Six buns, please.

4

Six pots of jam, please.

5

A big box of nuts, please.

6

Here's the bus! Here's Tom! Buns – yum yum!

Listen and point to the words.
Point and repeat.
Listen and say the number.

What's the time?

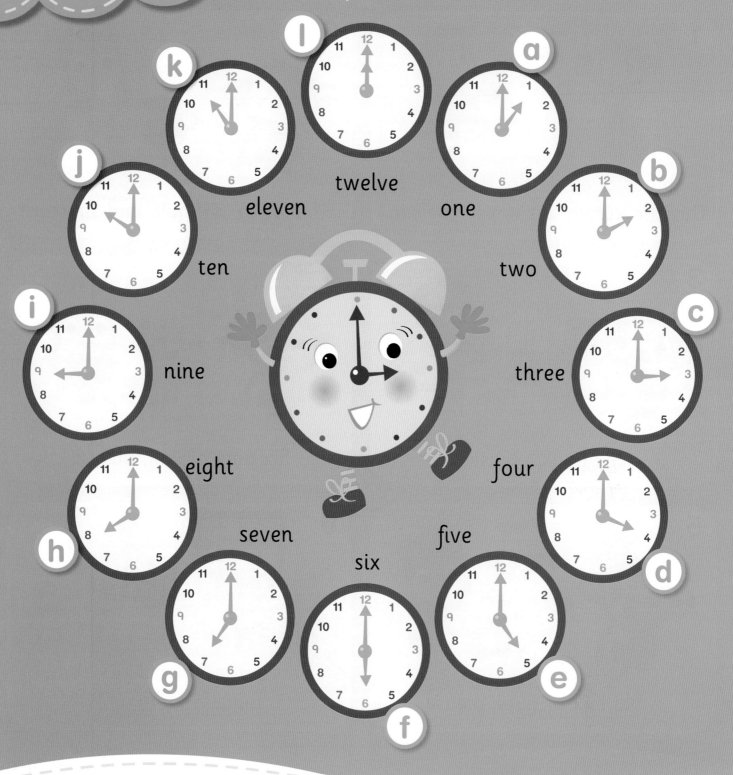

l twelve
a one
b two
c three
d four
e five
f six
g seven
h eight
i nine
j ten
k eleven

 1

 2

PSHE

Listen, point and repeat.
Listen, count and say the time.

 About me!

Have you got a clock in your bedroom?

Hide and seek

It's sunny.

One, two, three ...

Where are they?

They're next to the house.

No, they aren't.

We're behind you!

Listen, point and repeat.
Listen to the story.
Act out the story.

 About me! Do you play Hide and Seek with your friends?

Unit 6
Lesson 1

My town

I me of the want

in am on can a let's from and

1 2
shops   library   supermarket

super

museum   cinema   café   pool

3 4

I can ...

1 Listen and chant.
2 Listen, point and repeat.
3 Listen.
4 Listen and answer.

34

New Words

I can say my address.

Where do you want to go?
To the museum.

Let's go!

Listen, point and repeat.
Listen.
Listen and sing.

Grammar *Where do you want to go? To the museum!*

About me! What's your favourite place in your town?

Uu

1 m → u → m   mum

2 y → u → m   yum

3 r → u → g   rug

4 h → u → g   hug

5 m → u → d   mud

6 h → u → t   hut

7 b → u → n   bun

8 m → u → g   mug

9 r → u → n   run

Listen and point.
Listen and repeat.
Listen, point and say.
Listen. Find and say the number.

Pup in the mud

1

I'm Mum in the hut.

2

I'm Pup. I can run!

3

I'm Pup in the mud.

4

I'm Pup on the rug.

5

A mug of milk and a bun.
Yum yum!

6

And a hug from Mum!

Listen and point to the words.
Point and repeat.
Listen and say the number.

37

Left, right, straight on

Straight on.

Turn left.

Turn right.

 **1**

   2

 PE

Listen, point and repeat.
Listen and play.

 About me!

Do you know left from right?

Review

1

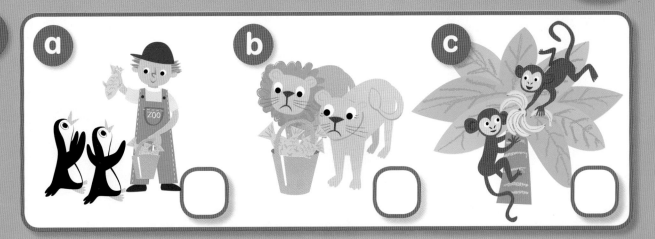

a b c

a b c

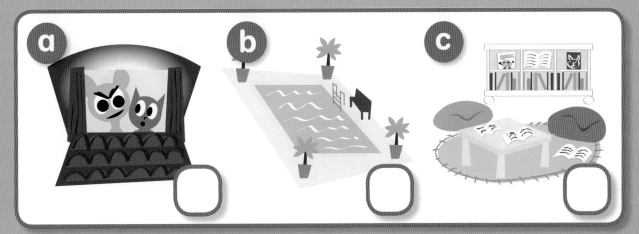

a b c

2

1

2

Review

Listen and tick.
Listen, point and say.
Assess progress with
Teacher's Guide.

39

Unit 7 My favourite clothes
Lesson 1

1   **2**

my are me is like the no we want I

it a can

swimming trunks

3

sandals

shirt

jeans

armbands

swimsuit

dress

4

I can ...

New Words

I can get dressed by myself.

1 2 3 4

40

Listen and chant.
Listen, point and repeat.
Listen.
Play.

5

6

What are you wearing? My hat.

 **7**

5 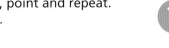 **6**

Listen, point and repeat.
Listen.
Say.
Sing.

7 Grammar *What are you wearing? I'm wearing …*   About me! What are your favourite clothes?

41

sh

①

sh → i → p
ship

②

sh → o → p
shop

③

sh → u → t
shut

④

sh → e → ll
shell

⑤

sh → o → r → t → s
shorts

⑥

sh → e → l → f
shelf

⑦

d → i → sh
dish

⑧

s → p → l → a → sh
splash

⑨

f → i → sh
fish

①  ②  ③  ④

Listen and point.
Listen and repeat.
Listen, point and say.
Listen. Find and say the number.

Is it a fish?

1 We want a big fish.

2 Hush! Hush! Sh! Sh! Sh!

3 Is it a fish? No. It's a shell!

4 Is it a fish? No. It's a shoe!

5 A ship. Splash!

6 The fish shop is shut. No fish in the dish.

Listen and point to the words.
Point and repeat.
Listen and say the number.

The four seasons

spring

summer

autumn

winter

 **1**   **2**   **3**

Science

Listen, point and repeat.
Listen and say.
Sing.

 About me!

Do you like very
hot weather?

Small waves and big waves!

1 I love summer.

2 I'm wearing my arm bands.

3 I can swim.

4 A small wave. Jump!

5 A big wave. Jump!

6 My hat!

1 Listen, point and repeat.
2 Listen to the story.
3 Act out the story.
4 Sing.

About me! What do you do at the beach?

Unit 8

Lesson 1

Jobs

I want me
look here
like is
my no

can on
for in
and
a not

1 **2**

firefighter

doctor

police officer

3

nurse

engineer

dentist

4

I can ...

New Words

I can clean my teeth.

1. Listen and chant.
2. Listen, point and repeat.
3. Listen.
4. Listen and answer.

5

6

I want to be a teacher!

7

Say after me ... a, b, c!

Listen, point and repeat.
Listen.
Sing.

Grammar *What do you want to be? I want to be ...*

 Do you want to be a teacher?

 47

8 Lesson 3 — ll ck

①
s → m → e → ll
smell

②
b → e → ll
bell

③
sh → e → ll
shell

④
h → i → ll
hill

⑤
f → i → ll
fill

⑥
d → o → ll
doll

⑦
b → l → a → ck
black

⑧
s → n → a → ck
snack

⑨
s → t → i → ck
stick

⑩
s → o → ck
sock

⑪
c → l → o → ck
clock

⑫
d → u → ck
duck

Listen and point.
Listen and repeat.
Listen, point and say.
Listen. Find and say the number.

48

Duck is ill

1
Look! A stick! I can spell duck.
D-u-ck. D-u-c-k. Duck!

2
Look! A clock on a rock.
Tick-tock! Tick-tock! Tick-tock!

3
Look! A sock on a rock.
A sock for a duck!

4
The snack is in the red bag.
Quack! I want a snack! Yum yum!

5
My tum! My tum!
Run up the hill. Tell Mum.

6
I'm not well. I'm ill. My tum!
Here's a hug for you.

Listen and point to the words.
Point and repeat.
Listen and say the number.

My teeth

I clean my teeth every day.

Brush your teeth well!

toothbrush

toothpaste

I drink water. I eat fruit and vegetables.

I don't like sugar!

I go to the dentist.

Open wide!

 ①

 ②

 ③

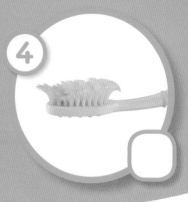 ④

①  ②   ③

PSHE

Listen, point and repeat.
Listen.
Look and draw:
✓ = clean ✗ = dirty.

About me! What colour is your toothpaste?

I want to be a doctor

I want to be a doctor.

Look at me!

Oh no!

Sit down, Lily.

Thank you, Tom.

You're a good doctor!

Listen, point and repeat.
Listen to the story.
Act out the story.

 Do you like going to the doctor's?

Unit 9
Lesson 1
Transcript

1 2

plane

helicopter

boat

AIRPORT STATION

train

airport

the like we I is with are look no my

in on a for can

taxi

coach

bus

3

4

I can ...

I can wear my seat belt.

New Words

1 Listen and chant.
2 Listen, point and repeat.
3 Listen.
4 Listen and answer.

52

We can go home by bus or by taxi.

Here's Horsey!

Thank you, Horsey!

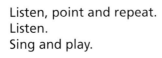

Listen, point and repeat.
Listen.
Sing and play.

 Grammar

We can go by …
or …

 About me!

Do you like trains?

ch   th

1 ch → i → ck

2 ch → i → p
chip

3 ch → i → ck → e → n
chicken

4 ch → i → n
chin

5 l → u → n → ch
lunch

6 m → u → n → ch
munch

7 th → i → n
thin

8 th → i → ck
thick

9 b → a → th
bath

10 p → a → th
path

Listen and point.
Listen and repeat.
Listen, point and say.
Listen. Find and say the number.

The three chicks

1. Chicken is in the bath with the three chicks.

2. Chips for lunch.

3. 'We like chips,' say the three chicks.

4. Look! Thin Fox is on the path.

5. No chicken and chicks for lunch!

6. Ouch! My chin!

Listen and point to the words.
Point and repeat.
Listen and say the number.

Sink or float

float

sink

Science

Listen, point and repeat.
Look and say: sink or float?
Try the experiment. Use a
plastic and metal spoon.

About me!

Can you float in the swimming pool?

Do boats float?

Do boats float? Yes.

Boats are big.

Can we go by helicopter?

I like the boat.

I can see a train.

Ice creams! Thanks, Dad.

 1 2 3   4

Listen, point and repeat.
Listen to the story.
Act out the story.
Sing.

About me! Would you like to go on a boat?

57

Little Red Riding Hood

the
I we my of
with says
want are
here

and | stop
not a on for
up let's it
get in lots

I'm Little Red Riding Hood.

I'm the wolf.

I'm Grandma.

We're flowers and birds.

Listen, point and repeat.
Listen.

You're not my grandma.

Help!

Go away.

Thank you.

We can ...

We can work together.

Stop the bus!

1

A snack for lunch! Here's the bus!

2

Bob and Gus are on the bus.
It's wet. 'Stop the bus,' says Gus.

3

Umbrellas up! Let's jump!

4

Bat with a mat, Rat with a hat, Thin
Fox and Fat Cat get on the bus.

5

It's windy. 'Stop the bus,' says Gus.

6

Run up the hill!
Let's play with the kites!

60

1 Listen and point to the words.

A duck, three chicks and Pup get on the bus.

It's hot! 'Stop the bus!' says Gus.

Look for shells in the sand.

We want a fish for the pan!

A snack for us. Lots of buns!

Let's run back to the bus stop! Goodbye!

Point and repeat.
Listen and say the number.

The school show

What do you do for your school show?

We play music.
We sing and dance.

We make puppets.

We paint big pictures.

We make masks.

a

b

c

 1

 2

 3

 Drama

Listen, point and repeat.
Listen.
Look and circle the odd one out.

Review

1

a   b   c

a   b   c

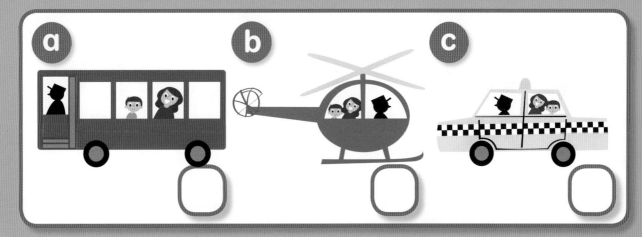

a   b   c

2

 1

 2

 Review

Listen and tick.
Listen, point and say.
Assess progress with
Teacher's Guide.

Well done! You're a Learning Star!